Conversationally Speaking:
WHAT to Say, WHEN to Say It, and HOW to Never Run Out of Things to Say

By Patrick King
Dating and Social Skills Coach
www.PatrickKingConsulting.com

As a show of appreciation to my readers, I've put together a FREE TRAINING VIDEO **(just enter your email address)** describing the BEST exercise for immediate social and romantic confidence. Click over to watch it now!

Table of Contents

CONVERSATIONALLY SPEAKING: WHAT TO SAY, WHEN TO SAY IT, AND HOW TO NEVER RUN OUT OF THINGS TO SAY

Introduction

I've been fortunate to have been exposed to a wide range of people that I would consider **role models**.

I have many of the typical ones that other entrepreneurs and authors do, but here's an unconventional one that might throw you for a curve.

Henry Kissinger.

First, some background.

Henry Kissinger is primarily known as an American **diplomat** who served under Presidents Richard Nixon and Gerald Ford. He went to Harvard, and currently runs Kissinger Associates, a consulting firm that brokers international negotiations and dealings.

So besides to an aspiring Senator, why exactly is he role model-worthy?

Well, his list of accomplishments has literally changed the

course of history. Let's take a look.

Introduce a policy called *détente* between the United States and the former **Soviet Union** at the height of the Cold War, which many historians consider the beginning of the end of the Cold War and mutual rising nuclear threat? **Check.**

Institute talks between the United States and **communist China** which eventually led to the recognition and formalization of relations between two nations, ending 23 years of poor relations? **Check.**

Oh, and negotiate the Paris Peace Accords to establish peace and end direct United States military involvement in **Vietnam**? **Check.**

His body of work speaks for itself, but it's really the manner and method through which he accomplished these feats that makes him a huge role model for me.

At his most basic level, Henry **Kissinger was a master communicator, negotiator, and people person.** This is how he was able to bring quarreling countries together no less than three separate times in history, and save literally millions of lives.

He was able to talk in ways that people would listen and see the benefit of his words. He knew just how to appeal to people's differing motivations and intentions to work out an understanding that never could have developed otherwise.

He broke political standstills and bridged ideological and philosophical differences in ways that both spared and ended great conflicts. He deeply understood how to bend people's positions to embrace reality and compromise.

Finally, he just made things happen through **sheer skill and will**.

Can you imagine having that much social grace that you can literally bend the fate of nations with your conversations? Me neither, but that doesn't mean it's not a worthy goal to strive for.

It's clear what the power of simple conversation can do – if it can shape history, just imagine how much more enriching it can help our **personal lives** be?

Conversation is the bedrock of any relationship, and it's exactly how and why you have bonded with every person in your closest social circles. There may have been some circumstantial luck involved from time to time, but my hope is that through the principles in this book, you will be able to strike up a conversation with anyone at any time, with nothing circumstantial required at all.

You'll understand how and why a conversation plays out the way it does, and see it for the science of **pattern recognition** that it really is.

I cover all phases of a typical conversation from icebreaking

to leaving on a high note, and nearly every part inbetween –
not just **WHAT** to say, **WHEN** to say it, and **HOW** to never
run out of things to say... but **WHY** everything works the
way it does.

You'll uncover a deep understanding of **social mechanics**
that will make you, conversationally speaking, prepared for
anything.

We might not be able to reunite the Koreas, but we can
definitely make a difference in how fulfilled we are on a
daily basis.

1. Master conversation; relationships.

What are your goals in **life**? Too heavy to start with?

Okay, so what are your goals for the **next week**? Is it work-related, hobby-related, or just social in nature?

Whatever you end up answering is not the important part – the important part is the realization that conversation and small talk is going to be **integral** to accomplishing it.

Our world is not ruled by strict requirements and objectivity, despite what we might like to believe. We don't live in anything remotely resembling a **meritocracy**, and the **relationships** you are able to cultivate are really what propel you forward in this life.

Thus, there's a logical thread here that I feel obligated to spell out.

Success requires as many strong relationships as you can create, and relationships are made strong by conversation that delves deep and allows two people to actually connect.

At its best, it allows people to drop all pretense, become vulnerable, and relate to each other in ways they never thought possible. This engenders love, friends, business, and accomplishments.

Beyond the benefits that becoming a strong conversationalist will give you, it's just a **necessity**. You just can't avoid social and interpersonal interaction unless you decide to become a shut-in... but even then, you have to occasionally order food or open the door for the deliveryman.

Unsurprisingly, most people are not naturals at conversation and social skills in general. When you walk away from an interaction thinking someone was awkward or made you uncomfortable, that's the exact indicator. We're never explicitly trained in these things the way we are in geometry, geography, and the capitals of every state in the country.

Gee, I wonder which one is actually more useful in the **real world**?

People also have various internal anxieties and mental blocks that might prevent them from successfully engaging people in conversation on a regular basis.

Regardless of the path that led you to this point of wanting help and improvement, rest assured and comforted that it will be an easier climb than you think. Like anything that is necessary, you might involve a bit of **kicking and screaming as you leave your comfort zones**, but there are some compelling reasons to do so.

First, conversation skills open trust.

The first meeting between two people can be **cautious and tense**. If you have not been introduced by friends and validated by the network effect, you simply don't know someone and whether or not you can trust them. If they'll betray you or be nice to you. If you'll get along or hate each other.

The first few moments are a quick haze of attempting to collect basic information with which to make an informed decision about trust, opening up, who to build relationships with, and who to ignore.

Initial conversation is an effective way of detecting each other's interest and most importantly, figuring out whether we could be comfortable with each other. Small talk may seem very superficial and rather innocent but in terms of interpersonal relationships, it's actually a very **important filtering mechanism**. It can give people the information they need whether they plan to let this person in deeper into their lives or hold them at a certain distance.

Small talk and conversation is really kind of a socially accepted gateway for you to let other people know what you're interested in, what's important to you, what your personality is like, and your personal twist or spin on common knowledge or current events.

With rusty or non-existent conversation skills, you run the risk of being perceived as someone that is untrustworthy, not worth spending time with, or just awkward.

Second, conversation skills make people feel safe.

Conversation can be as shallow as you want. But done correctly, it makes people feel comfortable and safe with you, and ultimately trust you.

Initial small talk and conversation is typically neutral in nature, and about harmless topics that most people can agree on. Anything else and it's not really small talk, it's just abrasive and off-putting in nature.

Yet still, there is the opportunity to provide context and information about who you are, what your values are, and how you conduct yourself so people can become comfortable and trust you. This small talk is the gateway to friendships, opportunities, and relationships.

When people feel safe, they reciprocate and attempt to draw you into their sphere of personal space. They'll share with you, and when you have two people sharing information, that is the foundation of trust and intimacy.

Our true friends are who we feel like will be there for us thick and thin. You don't get to that position just by standing next to each other silently, no matter how long you have stood. Friendships and relationships are a series of shared moments and connections, driven by conversation.

Ergo, upgrade your conversation quotient and capacity, and find yourself at the cusp of many more deep relationships and friendships.

2. Everyone likes a verbal mirror.

There's a saying that essentially states that the best way to engage people is to let them talk about themselves. Give them the space to explain their motivations and intents, and no one can resist the temptation of talking about **their own cleverness**.

Coming from a **date coaching background**, I can tell you that the same advice holds true because it has the same goal. On a date, it's not a bad rule of thumb to do the minority of the talking, and allow your date to talk about themselves and their thoughts.

We innately know that this has the effect of driving a conversation because people like to talk about themselves. It also gives the appearance of a smooth, flowing conversation because both people are driving the conversation along and working together **for a single purpose – to talk about the other person**. The end result is that the other person will just like you more, because they have perceived a great conversation to have taken place.

So… do you find yourself clamming up when you meet new people? Nervous and anxious with others?

Then become a verbal mirror. **Shine the conversation back onto the other person and see your interactions blossom.**

Most people have a certain amount of mental blocks in dealing with people that they don't know or have just met.

But they will love to engage on topics that they are comfortable on or experts on… and who isn't an expert on **themselves**?

If there is any one thing about human nature you need to learn, people love to talk about themselves. **The average person navigates the world with themselves as the center.** They process the information the world gives them from their own personal perspective.

Piggyback on this common tendency so that they basically do all the work when you're talking to them. Your job is to read the signals carefully so that you can change the direction of the conversation so that they can keep talking. And the funny thing about all of this is that the better you are at listening to people, the more they would think you are a great conversationalist. Pretty **paradoxical**, right?

Conversations tend to suffer as a result of people feeling that they are in the **spotlight**. Like they are performing, and waiting to be judged for what they say. That they are in the center of the room and everyone's eyes are on them and making them incredibly **self-conscious**. People clam up and this is the exact phenomenon when you just can't think of anything to say to someone.

The truth is you're a good conversationalist. You just let the pressure of having to perform get the best of you. This is when anxiety about performing kicks in because you have a very human and common place fear. What fear is this? The fear of rejection. Nobody likes to be rejected. Nobody likes to be made to look like a fool. But the reality is that you already have those great social skills.

One of the best ways to train yourself to do this is to master the art of making the other person talk.

So when you meet a new person and structure and direct the conversation based on what's important to them, you have yourself an instant conversation – the best part of it is that there's no heavy work on your part. There is no need for you to feel that you are performing because the conversation is all about them, and they feel the same way in talking about something so comfortable to them as themselves.

It's very important then to focus on what your job is. A simple mindset shift can help you here.

Your job during conversations is not to grab the spotlight and come up with something profound, witty, intelligent, or funny. You're not in the conversation to teach or preach.

Dumb it down! Instead, your job is to guide the conversation. Throw yourself in there from time to time to lure the person deeper into the conversation. The actual content, the actual meat of the conversation can be provided by the other person.

The better you are at guiding, the safer you feel and the less anxious you get about talking to people. Eventually, a sense of momentum kicks in, and you can pretty much talk with anybody because the reality is regardless of whether they live on the other side of the planet or a small corner of the United States, everybody is the same. Everybody loves to talk about themselves.

The more practice you have of luring people in talking about a common topic, to lure them in and have them basically take over the conversation with you guiding them at certain stages, the more confident and at ease you would feel around strangers and with any topic.

This can mean the difference between a high-performing sales person, and somebody who can't sell anything even if his or her life depended on it. This can also mean the difference between meeting the person that you're destined to live the rest of your life with and dying alone. The stakes are pretty high.

Great conversations really are all about **call and response** –

people cannot resist the call of talking about themselves. First focus on these topics and transfer the feeling and practice you get from them.

Key phrases:

1. Tell me more about _____.
2. Oh? How did that affect you?
3. How did you come up with that?
4. [Repeat the last few words of what they just said and trail off...]
5. Why did you think of that?
6. What was the best or worst part of that?
7. Why do you think that happened?

3. Icebreaking, melting glaciers, and starting a conversation.

When faced with a roomful of people we don't know, it's a threatening situation for almost all of us. How do we pick one person out, engage them, and break the ice with them?

It's an **inherently uncomfortable** situation that makes us a fish out of water. We don't want to disrupt people that might be having a nice talk with someone else, because we know that we've been annoyed when random people have butted-in. We don't want to say the wrong or awkward thing that will start an interaction off on the wrong foot.

Most of all we just don't want to be **rejected**! However, as with all things that hinge around the fear of rejection, realizing that **judgment is far less prevalent than you think** can do wonders. In other words, once you can get over the mental blocks of getting rejected from a conversation (which, honestly, doesn't happen much at all), you'll realize that it's just a matter of opening your mouth and doing it.

Of course, there are optimal ways to do it so that you can start off an interaction as easily as possible, and that's what I'll talk about here. Almost all (appropriate) icebreakers are welcome, but not all icebreakers are created equally.

Talk about what you have in common at that moment.

Even if you're somewhere that you've never been before with a group of strangers, there are bound to be commonalities. For starters, you're all at the same **location**, aren't you?

Social events always have themes and commonalities that you can draw on to icebreak conversations. If it's not a birthday party or college reunion, what is the one reason that brought this seemingly random group of strangers together? Is it a kickball party?

It can be as basic as a network of friends inviting their friends and friends of friends to hang out at somebody's house. You can talk about the friends you have in common. You can talk about the fact that you are in this interesting new house, and that you got invited a certain way.

What's important is for you to clearly identify what most people in that particular social space have in **common**. Search deep and you'll find it. From there, you can branch into actual conversation and learn about what makes people different.

To sum it up, **start with a broad commonality, then narrow into the opposite**. Focus into people's specific traits after breaking the ice with a shared reality.

Key phrases:

1. How do you all know the host?
2. It's my first time at this bar... is it always this rowdy?
3. Check out that wall décor, it's so funny.
4. So everyone here plays kickball? Who has the most powerful leg?
5. Host's house is so new, isn't it? I'm so jealous.
6. Where do you think they got the name for this bar?
7. Why do you think that guy over there isn't wearing shoes?

Lead the conversation to them after breaking the ice.

Recall in the precious chapter that everyone likes a **verbal mirror**. There may be no greater pleasure than talking about ourselves and explaining in detail our motivations in our daily lives.

Also recall that this opens people up, and makes them perceive you as a friend even if you just met. If you can probe people about themselves and find a topic relating to themselves, you can encourage them to stray onto that tangent.

Once you identify that, keep dwelling on it so that they can basically talk more and more about that particular topic. The goal here is a smooth transition from your icebreaker into a conversation with actual substance and connection.

A rule of thumb here is that you will probably be required to do 75% of the leading and talking at the beginning of an interaction. You will need to fill the silences yourself.

Sample question chain:

1. Did you see that cow head mounted on the wall? This place is crazy!
2. I've only seen something like that in Texas before, have you been?
3. Oh, where were you born?
4. New York definitely doesn't have cows like that. Why did you move here?
5. I've heard that the agriculture job market is strong here, but I never knew exactly what that meant. What exactly do you do within it?
6. So it sounds like a job that provides a nice level of work-life balance. Is that what you were looking for?
7. Great! Where's your next vacation? I just went to Thailand and highly recommend it.

From a general observation of the décor, to asking about where someone originated from, to deeper motivations and desires in a short series of questions.

Avoid controversy.

While I don't generally tell people to spout generalities like the weather, there is a time and place for conveying your opinion and standing out above the fold.

Icebreakers with people that you do not know are hardly the place for that. Your opinions can often be polarizing, which is not a negative thing. But given that your goal here is simply to **begin an interaction and make them comfortable with talking to you**, being the slightest bit abrasive won't help that goal.

Most topics can be talked about freely, but what makes them controversial is having **too strong of an opinion** on them, and immediately conveying that to others.

Keeping the goal in mind of beginning an interaction – what happens when you run across someone whose views don't line up with yours? You will be seen as an enemy or at least unpleasant person, as most people are **unable to separate** a civil disagreement with personal vendetta.

It doesn't really matter how you handle the situation of conflicting views. When this happens with someone you just meet, it's instinct to write them off because you don't know about them other than the fact that you butt heads philosophically. If you find yourself here, the conversation might not be salvageable.

So stay away from potentially dangerous topics like religion, politics, race, gender politics, or other divisive issues. You can bring them up, but don't offer your opinion on them until you gauge how the other person reacts, if at all.

If it appears that you might agree philosophically, then feel free to offer your unfiltered opinion. But that would be the exception rather than the rule.

Note details and provide your own.

You might be detecting a theme that conversations require some effort and thinking on your feet. You can't just coast in a conversation and expect that your autopilot responses will produce the connections that you want.

Taking note of details that the other person provides you with is an instance of where you can't coast, and you must **actively be listening** to the other person.

Mentally catalog some important details or aspects of a story that appear to excite your conversation partner, and return to those in times of doubt or impending silence.

By details, I mean like their hometown, occupation, hobbies, and other personal information they have divulged to you – things that they can relate to or that made their faces light up when they were brought up.

This way, you will always have something to talk about and instantly inject energy back into the conversation... as well as avoid awkward lulls and silences. You may not know that much about them, but **you should be able to detect what a person might be interested in and excited about within a few minutes**. Maintain interest and focus by focusing on them.

On your side, you should reciprocate with personal details and stories when appropriate. If you have a personal story that relates to a person's interest or context, it will draw them to you and make them view you as a person with more inherent value.

Key phrases:

1. Wait, you're from Philadelphia? So you're a big sports fan?
2. Did you mention earlier that you had seen this movie before?
3. I told you that I'm also from Pennsylvania, right?
4. I forgot, did I imagine that you said you used to play basketball?
5. Can we hold on a second and go back to the fact that you used to play basketball in college?
6. I can't believe that we are from the same tiny country in the Caribbeans!

These phrases fill any lull or silence easily.

4. Common questions and uncommon, better answers.

What was the last way that you greeted someone that you came across?

Was it some variation of "Hey," "How are you," or "What's up?"

And did you actually listen to or care what the response was going to be?

No? That's because these greetings and common beginnings to conversations are so overused that they are basically **instinct**. They fade into nothing and don't leave anyone with an impression whatsoever. If you want a one-liner conversation, well that's pretty easy to accomplish.

Obviously, this is not our goal with this book.

Look at the common questions and greetings that you'll be asked as **softballs** – by which I mean they are gifts given to you because they are so easy to answer in uncommon and interesting ways. Start preparing and answering these questions with great **stories and phrases**, and you will instantly captivate whoever you are talking to.

The best part about this chapter's lesson is that it is something that you can prepare for **beforehand**. So much of conversation is stressful to us because it depends on a certain amount of skill and thinking on your feet – this can be daunting because we often imagine ourselves running out of things to say and simply standing there dumbfounded.

If you can take some time to prepare answers and stories for situations that you know will come up in each conversation you take part in, you can **eliminate** a large part of the fear!

As I touched on above, the most common conversation starters are simply variations of "How are you," or "What's up." There is nothing special about these questions, and they are simply ways that people (1) acknowledge you, and (2) show an interest in your life.

Unfortunately, we routinely fail to take advantage of the openings that we are given on how to engage people. Some answers can lead to engaging and entertaining conversations, while most simply cut conversation short.

You are definitely familiar with the latter. They don't ask for more information. They respond and block off the other person. "I'm fine, thanks!" "Great." "Good, you?" "Great! Bye!"

Nothing about that exchange is compelling or will lead to any kind of connection. All conversation killers basically revolve around giving a broad yet vague answer.

Easy solution – **respond with answers that lead to more questions**.

If you want to engage the person in a deeper conversation, you cannot give an answer that cuts them off.

When you give this kind of answer, this opens up the conversation in many different directions. The conversation can talk about travel stories. It can talk about any discrepancies between travel brochures and actual travel experiences.

Responses that lead to more questions are more effective when they start with a story. When somebody asks you a very broad and often banal question, you can choose to say, "I'm great," and just cut it off, or you can throw in a personal story. When you tell them that you just got back from Rome or Paris, it attracts their curiosity and you can start an exchange of travel stories, which can lead to many different tangents.

You have to start with your story because it makes the conversation more **personal**. This draws them in. When they're drawn in, they start throwing in their story, and then you can use that technique that I've mentioned earlier of putting the spotlight on them if you're feeling awkward or anxious. You only need to ask **follow-up questions** to dig deeper into their story and basically the conversation will take a life of its own.

The art of great conversations is not a mystery. It's about looking at the common humanity you have with the person you're talking with and letting the story take over. Everybody has a story, and human nature is set up in such a way that everybody is in a rush to tell their story.

As long as you know these facts, you can then use them to your advantage to become a great conversationalist.

5. Effective listening in three steps.

According to a recent statistic, most **marriages** in the United States break down not because of infidelity or money issues, but **failure to communicate**. While this might seem like a "duh" moment, it still underscores a few very important concepts about our daily lives.

First, the ability to engage people meaningfully in conversation and have it lead somewhere occasionally – as a general blanket statement, **people aren't good at it**. Even within the supposedly safe confines of marriage, people have issues with difficult conversations and the things that need to be said. I would assert that a large part of this aversion to marital conflict is because of either partner's inability to listen effectively.

Second, people don't listen well, and there's more to listening than just sitting quietly and waiting for your turn to speak. Communication issues arise when issues are miscommunicated... and when **a safe space isn't created** to allow grievances to come to light.

Third, people think they are communicating but aren't

really. They're so uncomfortable with all that genuine and open communication entails that they only dip their toes into the process. This means that half-messages are sent all the time, and nothing is completely understood because people just want to end the process.

That's why being a good listener is important.

Fortunately, there are three easy steps to set you on your path to being a great listener and subsequently great conversationalist. This goes beyond the strangers at the cocktail party – it can help salvage your relationship with your significant other.

Step one: ACTUALLY focus on the other speaker.

When you're listening, it means that your mouth is completely shut and there is nothing coming out of your mouth.

More important are the following two aspects: (1) you are not simply waiting for your turn to speak with something on the tip of your tongue, and (2) you are actually acknowledging and **digesting** what is being told to you.

Many people like to pride themselves as good listeners based purely on the fact that they let people rant about their lives. The act of sitting silently does not make a good listener, it just means they are good at nodding and saying "Uh-huh…" At the end of it all, the only person who feels good about that interaction is the person who thinks they are listening well, because the speaker won't be getting any value from it.

Real listening is all about focusing on the speaker. This is very hard for many people to swallow because most people are egocentric. Unfortunately, if that's how you handle your relationships, you're not going to get far. If that's how you conduct yourself at work, you probably aren't going to get promoted.

You have to learn how to focus on the speaker. Instead of thinking about your trials and tribulations and what's happening in your life, wrap your mind instead around the life of somebody else. Wrap your mind around what's important to them and focus closely on the collection of ideas, emotions, and revelations coming from the speaker.

This may seem easy, but it isn't. A lot of people think that they're good listeners when, in reality, they're **filtering**. So the person is talking but they're only listening to the things they want to listen to. They're only getting the message that they want to get. This is not real listening. **Real listening is a raw feed**.

Step two: follow up.

As I said before, effective listening isn't just sitting there quietly.

It's **acknowledging and taking words in, synthesizing them, and formulating specific feedback and follow-up**.

What is NOT a real follow-up? "Uh huh," "Oh, I see," and "Oh my God!"

A real follow-up question is when you put yourself in their shoes and try to understand the details they have to deal with. If you're talking to somebody that just lost his job, put yourself in that **emotional state**.

How would you be feeling when you have your home mortgage due the next month, and you lost your job? How would you be feeling when your kids come home, and they see that their daddy doesn't have a job anymore, right?

That's what your questions should revolve around. The center of gravity must be on what is important to the speaker, and the conversation should flow from there. Many people think that they are good conversationalists because they basically think they already have the answer. These conversations tend to be one-sided and ultimately, useless.

By focusing on the speaker and practicing empathy, you can then tease out information that could actually help them because most people's problems are solved by answers that are already contained within the question. You ask follow-up questions, you have to place it from their perspective and what matters to them.

A great conversation is a journey, not the destination. It's not a mad rush towards this fixed answer that doesn't change. Instead, it's really just about the process the person just letting their emotions out, picking through the details, and really having another person be there to **share the experience**.

Step three: fight the urge to talk about yourself.

My last breakup took a mental toll on me because I had invested so much into the relationship. Despite that investment, I knew it had to end at some point and just couldn't see it culminating in marriage.

So I took the news to my best friend and really just wanted to unleash everything that was in my heart and head at that point.

What transpired was incredibly frustrating. I would talk about the aspects of the relationship that weren't working for me, and made me reconsider my entire life course.

Then she started talking about how she did that with her husband, and then how her husband's family went on a trip to Israel that past summer. And then how that trip was horrible, and led to some family discord. **She stole my damn thunder.**

Normally I'm more than a willing ear, but this was a low

moment for me and she failed to recognize that she needed to kick her listening mode into gear. She flipped the focus of the conversation from me to her in a frustrating series of side thoughts and thinking out loud.

Your job is to give them **safe emotional space** where they can explore ideas, be honest with feelings, and otherwise come up with a sense of clarity. You flush all these **down the toilet** when you talk over them or switch the focus of the conversation to yourself.

This goes beyond stealing the thunder, and serves to make the other person feel **marginalized** and unimportant. Real listening is about the speaker and not you. They're the ones who know the answers regarding their problems not you. So it's really important to fight the urge to dominate the conversation.

Listening doesn't take an advanced degree, but it takes a lot of heart, empathy, and compassion.

6. Building a bulletproof first impression.

When meeting someone new, we've all had that moment of "No, thanks," right off the bat, haven't we?

I have, and I don't think I'm more judgmental than the average person.

The reason that happens is because that person made a **negative first impression**. You just didn't like their "**vibe**" or their presence – and that's exactly what the first impression governs.

It doesn't really matter who you are or what your goals. You simply need to know how to make a better first impression. We only get one shot at this until the opportunity is gone. Once that happens, everything else you do or say will be viewed through the lens of that negative or lukewarm impression, and it's a pit that is extremely difficult to climb out of.

The good news is that it's not as difficult as you may think.

Part of the reason that people make really bad first

impressions is that they come into a social situation with a lot of **anxiety or fear**. If you go into a social situation looking to impress people or prove a point, nine times out of ten, you'll drop the ball.

Remove the fear of judgment from your mind and see your first impressions soar. Of course, that's easier said than done, so in the interim, a set of basic guidelines can cover your bases.

<u>Make eye contact.</u>

In **western** culture, eye contact establishes trust and credibility.

Accordingly, the **lack of eye contact** can convey many things. It can mean that you're being evasive, or have something to hide. It can also convey that you are weak person and basically looking to be dominated. There are all sorts of meanings that people can read into your inability to make eye contact.

Awareness is half the battle here, as eye contact is not typically a difficult step for people to internalize.

Don't stare into their eyes like you are trying to read their soul. That just creeps people out. This relates to my next point.

<u>Smile with your eyes.</u>

As mentioned above, you have to make eye contact, but there are objectively better ways to do it.

The best and most comfortable way to do it is to smile with your eyes. Your eyes are not just dead pools or black, blue, brown, or green.

In other words, your eyes are communicating to the person you're looking at that person is welcomed. It's communicating to that person that you're open for an exchange or conversation.

However, if you do it wrong, and you just look at somebody straight in the eye without smiling with your eyes, this can be viewed as a challenge or a threat. It can be viewed as showing dominance. Not a good move if you're trying to make a sale or meet somebody new.

How do you smile with your eyes? Lift your eyebrows (which makes you appear non-threatening and empathetic) and crinkle your eyes around the edges. Incidentally, the easiest way to crinkle your eyes thusly is to genuinely smile, so that's a two for one tip.

<u>Use an expressive voice.</u>

Many people don't know it, but they don't convey anything close to what they want to because they don't have an expressive voice.

It's the difference between being good at **sarcasm**, and coming off like an asshole most of the time.

Many **foreign students of English** embody the difference, as they can say phrases and words fine, but without proper expression and inflection. The meaning falls flat and sometimes is taken the opposite way.

You want to be seen in a positive light immediately upon first impression, so express positivity through your voice. Done?

Now use ten times the amount of positivity that you think you just used. **Exaggerate it**, because chances are that what seems like a lot to you isn't much in reality.

Don't take the chance of being misunderstood or misconstrued in a negative light. Practice your expressive voice to convey exactly what you want.

Focus on your similarities.

There is an inherent human bias to people who are similar to us. We open up better to people who look like us, sound like us, and speak the same language as us.

So when you talk to somebody new and want to make a great first impression, always look for similarities and focus on those. Instantly, you will be seen in a positive light, as the person will see themselves in you – and **who doesn't like themselves**?

Focusing on your similarities will make people less apprehensive and open themselves to you in a far deeper manner than they would otherwise. It's like you are their neighbor, and who doesn't want to endear themselves to their neighbor?

Reflect the emotional cues of the speaker.

Want to make a great first impression? Laugh at someone's jokes or curse the traffic just as they do.

Is this fake or insincere? No.

Here's why.

You're not lying or conveying something that you don't feel, you're just increasing the amount of social lubricant in a situation. Here's another interpretation: isn't it **common sense** to remain somber when someone is telling a sad story and express anger when someone else wants to rant about something?

When this person gets the impression that you get them on an emotional level, they are willing to let you in further in terms of emotional intimacy.

Send the right body language signals.

Awareness is half the battle on this one. You don't have to send body language signals of attraction or affection, but you **DO have to avoid sending out negative or closed off signals**.

Guys who are unable to pick up women at singles' bars usually fail because of this. They're mouths are saying one thing, their face is saying another, and their body is saying another. Whole communication – your words, the way you say your words, the tone of your voice, your body language, and your facial expressions – must be **consistent**. Don't send the wrong body language signals because it sabotages the kind of intimacy and trust that you're trying to build.

Beware of how you cross your arms, stand or lean back to appear standoffish, your facial expression while listening, how much you cover your face, fidget, and which direction you point your toes in. They all contribute to a **consistent image** of how engaging a person you appear to be.

Making a great first impression really involves **both verbal and non-verbal signals**. To sum it all up, you really need to have a high level of consistency so whatever signals that you are sending can lead to higher levels of intimacy, confidence, and trust and are not sabotaged by non-verbal signals.

7. Tell stories like Homer and Aesop combined.

Is there anyone that sticks out in your memory as a great conversationalist?

Nine times out of ten, the reason why you were so impressed by these people is because they told **great stories**.

Conversation is really a set of interesting remarks and related stories, so it's no wonder that great storytelling can make your conversation skills skyrocket. It's a **cornerstone** of how we actually communicate with others.

<u>Focus on the central point of the story.</u>

If you want to be a better storyteller, figure out the **central point** of the story before you tell it. What is the central idea you're trying to communicate? The clearer this is to you, the better you will communicate that idea.

All details must lead to this central point and be somewhat related. If you have to ask yourself why you are mentioning this person or detail, then it only serves to dilute your story and message. Think of the central point as the **thesis** of the story – every detail or point must relate to it, or provide context for it.

Poor storytellers have one thing in common: they talk on and on and really never get to the point. These stories are annoying because they take your attention and waste it – you can waste minutes on somebody that basically doesn't know how to tell a story.

The key to effective storytelling is that the details of the story that you're going to tell must lead to the central point.

For example, you are telling a story about **performing at an open mic** last week. Focus on the details of the setting, the performance, and the lead up to it. Talk about your feelings, and how much you like performing.

What **isn't** related to the central point of the story? Where you got your guitar, how much your mother likes your singing, and how bad the commute was to get there. Stay focused.

The central point must have an emotional payload.

Human beings are emotional creatures. We'd like to pretend that we're rational, or we make our decisions based on logic.

But nine times out of ten, we make an impulsive or

emotional decision then we later on justify by coming up with some sort of rational explanation. We're all emotional animals and there's nothing wrong with that.

This means that if you're going to tell a story, you have to make sure that there is an emotional payload. When people get to the end of your story, either they're laughing, they're crying, they're feeling angry, or any other emotional reaction.

For an effective story, **there has to be an emotional reaction at the end**. Either they feel uplifted and enlightened, or they feel outraged or moved to action, or their hearts have been moved to pity.

Otherwise, your story will simply engender a reaction of "So what?" or "...and?" or "Is that it?"

You have to ensure that the central point of your story has an emotional payload or other people would not find your story engaging or interesting.

Paint a picture.

Anyone can tell a dry and boring story.

All you have to do is describe what happens in steps. Reduce your story down to a series of actions, including a conclusion, and what do you have? A story that is as good as a set of instructions to do laundry with – equally as thrilling and emotionally moving.

Great stories are when the storyteller lets you smell what he or she smells in the story. **Great stories are when the colors are very vivid and vibrant**. Great stories take place when there is a lot of sound and dynamism in the details of the overall narrative.

You can tell a lousy story when the details are flat, when many of the details are rushed through, or otherwise missing. **It's as if you are there**. The better you are in painting a very palpable, vivid, and really engaging story, the higher the likelihood that this person would be emotionally engaged.

Great storytellers make great first impressions in social settings because they are great communicators. They are able to help us to connect better with our emotions and intellect. Great storytellers are few and far between, and this is why you need to really step up your game so you can master the art of conversation.

8. Making safe topics into failsafe conversations.

If you want to master the art of conversation, you have to know how to come up with conversation topics that can lead to great conversation.

Just kidding.

This is actually untrue and a damaging mindset, because it will make you depend on that magic topic that doesn't really exist.

What is the definition of a great conversation? Let's keep it simple. **A great conversation is a conversation that allows both people in the conversation to feel better about each other**.

Not all topics lead to great conversations. Some topics actually lead to dead-end conversations because they're so close-ended and simple.

As the title of this chapter says, **it is perfectly possible to take safe topics and twist them to your advantage**. It's all a matter of knowing how to move beyond the material provided and create a connection regardless.

Therefore, it is perfectly harmless to focus on what might be otherwise called boring small talk topics. The big benefit here is that you can bring them up with anyone and someone will have something to say about them. As long as you take a **personal and emotion-based angle** off something universal, you can twist it into a great opener to branch out into other topics that can lead to deeper credibility and trust-building.

Weather.

One of the safest topics to talk about is the weather.

The reason why this works time and time again is because it's a shared experience. If you live in the part of the United States where it snows a lot, everybody can agree that it's snowing. What makes this an interesting discussion point is that everybody has a different spin on the weather and what it means to them. For example, if somebody was caught in a snow storm on his way to the Bahamas, that's a great gateway for a great conversation about vacations.

Another way this can lead to conversation is when somebody talks about the humidity in their house leading to mildew that leads to home repair. This can be a great way to transition from talking about the weather to do-it-yourself construction projects around the house.

Weather is a great starting area or staging area where it can branch out to other personal areas that you have similar experiences with, and you can share information on.

The worst way to deal with a weather topic is to just say to the person, "Yes, I agree. It's bad weather," and leave it at that.

Weather is a great conversation topic because it's **open-ended and leads to many places**. Don't destroy its power by restricting it to a descriptive or objective discussion about the weather only and leaving it at that.

Current events.

Many current events topics can lead to interesting side discussions.

However, you have to be choosy about which current event you bring up, because many are inherently controversial and divisive.

If you talk about current events that focus on those categories, instead of a free ranging conversation where the people engaged in the conversation feel about each other and feel like they know each other a little bit better, it might divide. You might have an argument or a debate and this is precisely what you don't want.

Focus instead on current events like local news or any kind

of current events that is harmless and shapeless enough that it can lead to other personal topics.

Common personal experiences.

Everybody takes vacations. Everybody has gone to high school. Everybody has done certain things that most other people share.

Focus on these common personal experiences and branch out from there.

By focusing on what we all have in common, you can branch out the conversation to more intimate topics.

The key to harmless, safe topics is not to stay on them. You use them to start out conversations. You use these banal talking points, and then you draw the person in. You then get the other person to talk about something more personal. That's how you use harmless small topics to lead to great conversations.

9. Avoid awkward and uncomfortable silences.

One of the most painful situations known to man is the sinking feeling of an **awkward silence** during conversation.

You may have done all that you can to carry the conversation and engage the other person, but sometimes awkward and uncomfortable silences still pop up. This can give people the impression that you are a bad conversationalist, even if they are the one at fault, and even prematurely end conversations as people excuse themselves to **escape** the awkwardness.

But that's some amateur stuff. With a little bit of preparation and awareness that I will teach you, you should be able to avoid the vast majority of awkward silences within conversations. And subsequently, your conversation partner will walk away thinking that they had an amazing interaction with you.

Why?

It's the realization that most people's conception of a great conversation is **nonstop banter**. When you are able to minimize silences and lulls in a conversation, this is exactly the feeling that people are looking for – and when you give it to them, they will impart and assume many positive feelings to your interaction.

Okay, so what are some steps to minimize silences?

Learn to lead.

Most people that you will come across will not be gifted conversationalists. They depend on serendipity to make good conversation with new people. But this is not you.

You will take the lead in a conversation. Just imagine how an **interviewer** takes the lead in an interview. They are in a position of power, but more importantly, they act like it. They ask the questions, move the conversation along to different topics, and generally dictate the exact direction of the conversation.

You can do this whenever you sense a silence coming. Take the lead by preparing and taking notes of questions to ask or bring up whenever a silence comes, and take that opportunity to direct a conversation wherever you want it.

Assume the responsibility of filling every silence with **something that came up earlier in the conversation, or a clarifying question about something they said**.

Key phrases:

1. Wait, what did you say about [polar bears]?
2. Did you mention earlier that [you went to the University of Arkansas]?
3. I can't believe that you said [the University of Arkansas had a polar bear at one point]!
4. So anyway, [where were you born]?
5. Have you ever [been to Pennsylvania]?

<u>Dig deeper.</u>

When you engage a person in a conversation, you're basically saying "I find you interesting."

At least, in theory. But that's the mindset that you should be approaching people with. As such, you're interested in what they have to say, and the deeper motivations that drive them.

So you serve them a question, they'll hit it back to you... and then you should dig deeper to see what is behind their answer.

Underlying this aspect of conversations is the fact that the best conversations shouldn't be mechanical or surface. You shouldn't just be going through the motions. You should be sharing information that actually leads to greater understanding and emotional depth.

The key is to get that person to feel they know you on a

more intimate level. There is obviously a time and place for this, but being engrossed in this kind of discourse will either (1) make the silences thoughtful and more comfortable, or (2) kill them altogether.

Key phrases:

1. What did you mean by [insert phrase they spoke earlier]?
2. Why exactly do you think that?
3. Why did you go that route?
4. What was your thinking behind that?
5. Was that something you always wanted to do?
6. How did you get to that point?

Sum up their words.

People **hate** it when you put words in their mouth.

Which is why you should do it from time to time, especially to avoid silences and lulls.

If you sum up their words and you are correct in your summary, they will agree with you and clarify further.

If you sum up their words and are incorrect in your summary, they typically won't take offense. They'll take the **opportunity to explain** in depth what they actually meant.

This is a great way to get the other person to fill any potential silence, by compelling them to clarify something about themselves – this is often irresistible for people.

Key phrases:

1. So what I'm hearing is...
2. Let me get this straight... [repeat a sentence of what they said]?
3. Wait, are you telling me that [Argentina is tiny]?
4. What do you mean [...]?
5. Did you mean [...]?

Starting with taking the lead in your interactions, this collection of tips should keep awkward and uncomfortable silences at bay. The key here is either you filling the silence yourself, or making the other person feel compelled to fill it. Either way, it creates a more flowing conversation that most people associate with chemistry and friendship.

10. Bodily speaking.

It's easy to reduce conversation and all communication to the words that are coming out of our mouths. But that would be inaccurate and ignorant of what drives our every day interactions.

Emails — why do we use smiley faces and emoticons?

How can we use **sarcasm and many types of humor** if you were to depend entirely on the words that are coming out of our mouths?

Why do we use gestures to emphasize and maximize our emotions?

And of course, what about body language and how much does that communicate our messages?

Given all of the above, it shouldn't be surprising that only a **minority** of our overall message is communicated through our words.

You might be saying something with your mouth, but if your

body language is very different from the signals that you're sending, this can lead to confusion, mixed signals, and misunderstandings.

Human communication is all about consistency. Great conversationalists realize this and make sure that their cumulative signals sent are consistent with a message that they want. The tone of their voice, the facial expressions, the way they stand, the way their cross their arms, all these signals combine to amplify and strengthen the overall message that they're sharing.

This makes them a much more enjoyable person to be around because there aren't any lurking feelings of deception or **confusion**. What you see is what you get, and that's a comforting presence. Mixed signals make us feel like we're in the presence of a passive-aggressive roommate who keeps telling us to wash the dishes, except the dishes aren't yours.

This chapter should be viewed as a quick guide on how to (1) make sure that you aren't sending mixed signals, and (2) interpret other people's body language to ascertain their true meaning.

Here are quick small talk body language tips you should keep in mind to maximize your communication effectiveness.

Crossed arms.

When somebody that you're talking to has their arms crossed, it can signal a variety of things. The most common interpretation is that they are **protecting themselves** and holding their most important parts – their torso and organs. If you follow along this train of thought, it means that you have made someone at least a little bit uncomfortable, defensive, and insecure. They aren't opening themselves up to you or making themselves vulnerable.

It may not even have anything to do with you. But you can do a couple of things to open them up physically and conversation-wise.

When you actively ask them what their feedback is or what their insights are, you make them emotionally invested in the exchange, and you increase the likelihood that the conversation would be more of a two-way street.

Another way you can get somebody to uncross their arms is when you nod in agreement and give **big reactions of agreement** to their words. You're saying to them on a subconscious level that you're not an enemy. You're not there to threaten them or harm them, and you're on their side.

Finally, another way that you can deal with somebody that has their arms crossed when you're talking to them is when you ask them to tell a story. When you ask the person to tell a personal story, you're basically asking them to take the center stage in the conversation. This works wonders in terms of getting the person to feel that they have some level of emotional ownership over the conversation. They are invested in the conversation to a certain extent.

And of course, let this be a lesson to you in being conscious of how much you subconsciously cross your arms lest you come off **unapproachable and harsh**.

Leaning in and nodding.

These are separate body language signals, but often seen together.

Leaning in means exactly what you think it might mean. What do you do when you can't hear something that you want to? You lean in, and pay special and careful attention to it because you don't want to miss any of it.

So when someone leans in towards you, whether they are standing or sitting, it could possibly indicate that the conversation is going well and they value your input and further comments. They are engaged in the conversation, and actually interested in what's being discussed, and you.

Much the same can be said of a nodding person, where they are literally and figuratively agreeing with what you have said. They are **engaged and interested**.

Therefore the **lack** of a lean in or nod, or worse yet leaning back away from you, may be construed as disinterest and wanting the leave the conversation. If this is the case, you may be able to lure them back to engagement by asking them about their own personal story or opinion.

The challenge of dealing with somebody who's learning in and nodding is not so much to get that person to talk.

They are engaged for the time being, so you must take advantage of that momentary interest by asking questions and branching out the conversation to related subtopics to keep their attention. Make sure that your questions are more pointed or there's more variety in your questions so that this person can be engaged on the emotional, intellectual, spiritual levels.

They'll probably be open to answering somewhat more **personal and invasive** questions on account of how invested and engaged they are! Take advantage of this openness.

Body language is obviously a vast and expansive subject to cover in this chapter fully. In fact, I have an entire book on the subject and it only offers a broad overview with specific signals to watch out for.

In the context of conversation, body language can serve to complete a consistent set of signals that will ultimately make you appear more likeable and engaged, or the opposite. Much of the damaging body language we display is entirely **subconscious**, so take the awareness that this chapter provides you and try to observe how much other people in your daily life display it as well!

11. Social cues say more than your words.

Imagine that you've just received a screenplay with a great plot, fantastic characters, and a compelling twist at the end.

There's just one problem – there is **no narra**tion to set the stage or introduce the characters whatsoever.

You have no idea where scenes end and begin, how the characters are positioned, what they feel, or who anyone even is!

This is what an interaction is like without social cues.

Social cues (also known as hints, clues, signs, etc.) are small verbal and non-verbal hints that guide social interaction implicitly, and are used by most of us on an unconscious level on a daily basis. **They tell us what people are really saying**.

It turns out that we intuit so much of people's intentions, motivations, and emotions through implicit means such as facial expressions, body language, tone of voice, and even how close people stand to us.

Social cues, at their most basic level, act to **reduce the amount of ambiguity** in the communications we receive from others. It's why we can say something and mean completely the opposite – social cues will indicate otherwise and provide us an interpretation that allows for humor and sarcasm.

Given that most of us have had decades of practice in reading social cues at this point, it has allowed us to form a mental model of people's behaviors and intentions that serves us well. This is why we can say things like "I've got a bad feeling about her," or "I just knew he was thinking that!"

You just know it because you know what signs indicate it and also indicate the opposite. It's only when we are faced with the absence of them do we realize how important of a role they play in our lives.

The ability to recognize social cues and react accordingly is also precisely what the people we deem "**socially awkward**" lack.

A large part of social cues hinges on how socially aware and **observant** one is. You and I both know people that lack those traits. So what are some common social cues that you should be aware of?

Nodding.

Nodding, as you might expect, is a sign of agreement.

But you might not expect is that it's a sign of people making themselves agreeable to you. The difference is that while they might not explicitly agree with the words that you just said, they want to make themselves non-threatening and friendly to you. In either case, it's a sign of good vibes.

This social cue gives you the freedom to ask deeper questions and move the conversation to more intimate topics.

They mention it.

There's a rule in filmmaking that if you show an object by itself, you must return to it. The first time it is shown essentially **foreshadows** the direction of the film and the importance of the object.

It's pretty much the same way with conversation.

If your conversation partner mentions a specific person, event, or object, it's likely that they would like to turn the conversation to that topic. You shouldn't let the allusion slide, as it is probably in reference to something that they have a story about – and we know that stories are a great way for people to open up and feel comfortable with us.

This simple social cue requires you to pay more attention to what people are thinking inside, and how indirect people can be about their desires. Most aren't comfortable outright interrupting you or telling you that they want to talk about themselves, so it's up to you to pick up on this social cue to **allow them to talk about themselves.**

This social cue might also signal that you have been talking about yourself too much, and they want some of the spotlight. In any case, it will teach you to pay closer attention to the meaning behind people's words.

Key phrases:

1. Oh yeah, that totally reminds me of my trip to Mexico last summer. [at which point you should ask about their trip, and so on]
2. I did that last summer too in Japan! [ask about japan or their summer]
3. I've never been skydiving, but I did bungee jump a few times. [resist talking more about skydiving and ask about bungee jumping]
4. I actually met Tom Cruise once too! [ask about that fateful day]
5. Yeah, I actually made that apple pie! [ask about the damn pie and their baking prowess]

Similarly, they add a new detail or hint at a new story.

They're not bringing these specific references up just for their own entertainment.

Remember that people seriously enjoy talking about themselves. Give them that opportunity and they will enjoy the conversation that much more and ironically feel like they got more out of it.

With conversational social cues, we are trying to pick up on the subtle hints that will make our conversations flow better. A hallmark of this is simply being able to deduce what people want to talk about. If you can do this, you can simply make an interaction more pleasurable for the other party.

One-word answers.

Some conversations you just can't salvage.

If you find that every question you ask, even piercing, intimate, and intelligent questions are met with simple one-word answers and not much excitement or vocal inflection, read the writing on the wall.

This person is done with talking to you – don't be that person who overstays their welcome and pesters everyone, requiring people to rescue them from your presence.

If someone doesn't turn to face you when they answer you, consider your conversation doubly finished. They are attempting to show you that they are engaged with something or someone else, and that you should stop talking to them.

If you don't know people who awkwardly hang around conversations for too long, despite having nothing to contribute... then you may be that person. People don't like to outright reject others or tell them to go away, so you must look for the subtle ways people do this.

12. Exiting conversations with grace.

I've studied a lot of psychology in my life, and a phenomenon that simultaneously surprises me yet makes complete common sense is the **recency effect**.

The recency effect tells us that the most recent of an interaction, activity, event, or person that we are exposed to is what we remember the best.

This makes common sense because if we view the brain and memory banks as a **stack**, then it is completely logical that we can easier access items at the top of the stack, and things near the bottom of the stack get crushed or replaced.

It's surprising in a sense because it means that so much of what we do and say is simply invalidated as a result of the limited capacity of our memories. Even if we say or do the most charming of things, it is not guaranteed that people remember it because it isn't the last impression that people have of you.

Let's bring it back to conversation and how the recency

effect should dictate your actions.

You can be as conversationally fluent and charming during a conversation, but if you leave it in the wrong way, it can seriously skew people's perception of you in a negative way. If you had a great date yet fumbled the kiss by laugh-spitting on their face – it might not be the best impression left of you.

Moreover, if you leave a conversation in a negative way, it doesn't make people want to re-engage you at a later point.

<u>Give them opportunity to develop their story.</u>

Whenever you engage with others, there's always an opportunity there for people to tell stories.

We look at our experiences as a series of stories. Sometimes we experience things just for the story itself. Point being, we enjoy sharing our stories with other people, as stories are innately social.

Don't believe me? Do you ever post anything on social media? Then you're sharing a story.

So what happens if you share a particularly personal or funny story on social media, and people just don't seem to get it? Is that an experience that you're familiar with? I'm betting that you relish the opportunity to **set their minds right**.

It's the exact same in conversation. If people get only partway through a story that they are sharing, or if there appear to be misconceptions about the story that they don't have the choice to explain, they are going to walk away from an interaction very annoyed. The emotional payload or punchline is simply **ruined**.

Give them an opportunity to fully develop and finish their story, and then you can bow out of a conversation. To do so otherwise is to show misunderstanding of who they are, and they will assume that you misunderstood them.

Their stories might be lackluster, but it doesn't matter. What matters is that you're giving them enough opportunities to fully develop the story they have to share.

Deliver the feedback they are seeking.

Conversations only serve a few purposes, when you really break them down.

We engage other people for **entertainment, information, or pleasure** – if not presently, then for the hope of such.

We don't always seek these things consciously or knowingly, but there comes a distinct feeling of emptiness and dissatisfaction if we walk away from an interaction without fulfilling our purpose.

If you've ever been to a **networking event**, you might know the feeling. How do you feel if you talk to one person the whole night versus when you talk to 15 people throughout the night and collect all of their business cards. If you do the former, you will probably go home feeling like you didn't accomplish your goals.

So whether it is entertainment, information, or pleasure, try to hone in on what your conversation partner is seeking and give it to them.

How can you tell what they want? Let's simplify this.

Entertainment: They want to share their life experiences with you, or hear about yours. Listen to their story and ask follow up questions.

Information: They are asking you about something that you have special knowledge in. Give them a few actionable steps and resources to look up later.

Pleasure: They are flirting with you. Of course, this isn't something that you should feel obligated to satisfy them with.

A witty summation.

One of the most effective ways to end a conversation is to use a joke or some sort of witty comment that is open-ended enough that it can be the basis of another future conversation.

Of course, this requires a bit of thinking on your feet to get it right.

<u>Here are some examples that you can imagine saying while walking away</u>:

1. Well, interesting conversation on the bathroom habits of ants... I'll keep in the mind the tips you gave me!
2. Of course, Anna's friends would have a heated discussion about what kind of marketing strategy is best. I have so much research to do.
3. Wow, okay, I need to go look up and verify that fact... right now!
4. I'm going to go mention this to my friend over there, I think he will get a kick out of this.
5. Okay, my mind is blown by that fact. I need to decompress...
6. You guys are too crazy for me, I'm going to go see what those people are talking about.

Remember that the way you end your conversations reflects of how good a conversationalist you are – even if it doesn't. That's the irony of the recency effect.

13. Conversation killers.

Do you have a tough time carrying on a conversation? Do you often feel that your conversations often end sooner than they should end? Do you experience difficulty keeping a conversation going?

You might be committing any one of the following conversation killers without even knowing it. Yes, it might be **you** condemning your conversations to premature death.

Why do I point the finger at you?

Because you're the one reading the book right now, actively gaining the power to improve your conversations! Most people will never think about their conversations in such depth as I present to you, so it's up to you as the better conversationalist to lead and keep conversations interesting.

You're right.

Simply agreeing with someone is not saying much at all.

It says that you agree with the person. However, there is really **no meat** to the statement.

When you find yourself saying "You're right" a lot, you don't give the other person reason to keep pressing ahead with another story, or another insight or another observation. You just echo them, which isn't necessarily motivating. Even though people like to be agreed with, it can stop a conversation cold if there is no **additional insight**.

Instead, say, "I agree with you because X and Y."

When you lay out reasons, two things happen. First, you let that person into how you think. You give that person a sneak peek into how your mind works, how your mind handles logical processes. This is an opportunity for an intellectual level of intimacy. Second, when you explain the reasons why you agree with somebody; you are actually giving the conversation an opportunity to branch out to those areas.

Not saying "You're wrong."

Again, people like being agreed with. But if that's all the feedback they get from a conversation with no feedback or insight, they quickly get **bored** with praise alone.

People are less sensitive to judgment that you think. If you disagree with someone (tactfully and nicely) then rarely will they lash out at you. Note that there is a world of difference between respectfully disagreeing with someone and telling them that they are flat out wrong.

When you note to someone that you disagree with them, it spurs a certain level of **respect**, and from it, debate and discourse.

People will always relish the opportunity to explain their inner motivations and thoughts, so if you disagree with them, you give them opportunity to clarify and explain. Don't be a yes man/woman.

<u>Failure to ask follow up questions.</u>

One of the most common conversation killers is when you nod and after a person has said their piece and leave it at that.

You have to ask follow-up questions. If you truly agreed, there are certain areas that truly engaged you. You might want to focus on those areas by asking questions regarding points of agreement. This can increase the likelihood of the conversation branching out into subtopics that can lead to more stories and more shared information.

Remember that everyone is seeking one of three things from a conversation – entertainment, information, or pleasure. If someone has said their piece, without feedback it is impossible to feel fulfilled in an interaction. Follow up questions allow people to find their purpose satisfied.

14. It's an introvert's party too.

Introverts get an unfair rap in society.

Most of the time they are lumped together with the **socially awkward or anti-social**. We know people whose venn diagram does indeed intersect there, but they are the exception to the general rule.

The textbook definition of an introvert is one who recharges their **social battery** from spending time alone or otherwise with themselves.

It's pretty simple, actually. If you spend a day out with your friends at a barbecue, what do you feel more inclined to you when you return home? Crash and relax for the rest of the night, or regroup and join everyone else at a club?

Introverts would likely answer the **former**.

So introverts don't inherently have less of an **ability** towards conversation than extroverts do – they just have a lesser **capacity** for it. Unfortunately, life doesn't often care whether you are an introvert and have used up your social battery for the day. It will require you to push through, regardless of your level of fatigue.

Here are some conversation skills specifically designed for introverts who may be in need of just pushing through it occasionally.

Just introduce yourself.

Just do it.

Good conversations are a series of **sequences**. However, you rob yourself of the chance to start any of those sequences if you can't just be bothered to introduce yourself. It's the beginning of any conversation with a stranger, and often the biggest obstacle to overcome.

I know that as an introvert your social battery might have been exhausted hours ago, but this isn't a book that is going to not push you.

Part of social success as an introvert is seeing your social battery **extended and increased**, so actively making the choice to look around and think about who you can introduce yourself to – that's going to push your boundaries and make you more capable of seizing the opportunities that you might miss out on otherwise.

Passively participate.

So your social battery has run out and you still have to engage others. There's a relatively easy way to do this.

Just ask incredibly open-ended and personal questions to people. If I haven't made it clear already, people love talking about themselves. They will take any opportunity and opening to do so, especially those who are usually modest and humble about their accomplishments.

So if you just act like a mirror to them and ask them questions like this, you can participate in a conversation in a very passive manner. **Nod, smile, and ask.**

Prompt them to keep talking by asking questions like an interrogation – this is a very low effort way to interact with people.

The sweet irony is that this is also a way of interacting that makes people think that you are interested in them, and may work better in fostering relationships than active conversations.

Think out loud.

Part of the reason that introverts recharge their batteries alone is so that they can think their thoughts alone and in peace and silence.

We (yes, I identify as an introvert as well) like time to not have to answer other people and just reflect on the day. When we're alone, we go **deeper into introspection** than we would with other people, where every day situations wouldn't allow.

Oh, and not having to deal with others is a nice too.

But assuming that you can't muse on these topics with other people would be a fallacy. You will be supremely surprised when you simply **think out loud** about what you would usually muse on by yourself.

This is going to take your conversations to the next level in terms of introspection, information exchange, and pure interest.

The alternative is staying in conversations that are safe, shallow, and boring. The least you can do when your social battery is exhausted is to make things interesting for yourself, and thinking out loud on topics that you want.

Assume the other person is incredibly interesting.

If your social battery was exhausted, would that matter if your **favorite actor or musician** was at the bar next door?

I'm pretty sure that your reaction would be to at the very least 'suck it up' and participate in what appears to be a rare or once-in-a-lifetime situation.

What if you could **trick yourself** into thinking that in any situation, there is someone who is going to provide that much excitement or value for you?

Actually, it shouldn't be a trick because it's just the **truth**. Everyone is interesting, and everyone is better than you at something and can teach you something.

So here's the mindset: everyone is insanely interesting in their own way. Everyone is unique. The way they look at and experience the world is one of a kind, and it would be a shame if you deny this reality.

Let your curiosity and thirst for entertainment overcome your exhausted social battery.

If you expect that others have no value to provide you, you're both sabotaging yourself socially... and completely wrong.

Not everyone is a Nobel laureate, but then again neither are you.

As an introvert, I understand intimately how difficult facing large social situations can be. Sometimes I can fully admit to myself that I don't prefer large crowds, but does it matter if the choice is removed from my hand? It's up to me to make the best of it, and the tips I have here are designed to **extend and grow your social battery** so that no matter how tired you are, your conversation skills are still far above par.

15. Confronting without confrontation.

Not every conversation can begin and end with rainbows.

Sometimes conversations devolve into arguments and loud disagreements due to circumstances that are out of your control. You can avoid most of these.

But that's not what this chapter is about. This chapter is about the difficult conversations in our lives that we **can't** avoid – conflicts with people or situations in our lives that are necessary and unavoidable. We look at the world in different ways, and we can't all possibly agree on all things all the time. Criticism and disagreements will come up time and time again.

Confrontation is not a concept that the majority of us are comfortable with, and as a result we usually avoid it for as long as we can. But that just causes **resentment** and passive-aggressiveness to fester inside until it **explodes** in a mess of anger and emotion.

We all innately know that the best way to address an issue

is actually confrontation, but since we usually avoid it, we also don't know how confrontation works best. You can engage in a measured way that leads to an effective and efficient exchange of information and view, or you can simply verbally brawl.

You have to decide whether you'd rather engage in a productive conversation that leads to a resolution, or attempt to prove your point in sole pursuit of **being right**. The way you approach confrontation can either trigger an emotional outpouring, or a mutually beneficial exchange of ideas.

Like with everything else in life, there is an optimal way of proceeding that will make your difficult conversations and confrontations lead somewhere positive.

Create a sandwich.

Most confrontation and difficult conversations begin with **a simple criticism**. However, people deliver it in harsh ways that don't allow the criticism to be received in without defensiveness or other negative emotion.

One of the best ways to disarm people and their innate **defense mechanisms** is to create a criticism sandwich.

Just as a sandwich has **two pieces of bread around a piece a meat**, so should your criticism – except the bread should be positive statements, and the meat your criticism.

For example,

Bread: I really like how you're showing initiative and taking action with your daily tasks, Lisa.

Meat: However, I think that sometimes you tend to let this step over other people, and you can be a little pushy around them in your interest in pushing projects forward.

Bread: We've definitely seen some growth from your initiative, though. It's a good trait that is very hard to find in people these days.

You start on a positive note to make people feel comfortable and not defensive right off the bat. Insert your criticism in a tactful way, including the positive aspects of it. Then you end on a positive note so hopefully their respond is first to the positive note, and not directly to the criticism.

If you dive straight into the criticism, you will intimidate and threaten the other person immediately, and set the tone for the rest of the confrontation.

Focus on the consequences.

When you are confronting someone, you are rarely making a **judgment** about them. You are simply noticing something that you would like changed and bringing it to their attention so that they may fix it.

However, the difference here is going to be lost on most people. This is the reason that people become defensive and lash back at you when confronted and criticized. They feel that you are making a judgment on them and attacking them personally, which understandably is quite distressing to people.

That's why it is so critical to make clear that you are not criticizing them, hence striking the phrase "you're wrong," which is directly at them. Thus, you also should not directly criticize an action.

Instead, make it clear that you are only lamenting the **negative consequences** that are happening to you. It is not an attack on them, rather just pointing out how you are being negatively affected. More than likely, this will spur your conversation partner to turn on themselves and want to alter their actions to keep you from feeling that way.

If the person you're dealing with is intellectually honest, they can work from the faulty premises to come up with a logical conclusion that means them adjusting their actions.

For example,

"I keep having to park partially on the lawn as a result of our parking situation, which means that my pants and shoes get really muddy every morning. Would it be possible to shift your parking up a few yards every day?"

Instead of,

"Hey, you need to park better."

By stepping them through the analysis, they can see how they made the wrong turn and ended up with a conclusion that hurts you. Use their intellectual processes for them to come up with their own analysis. In other words, **they take ownership of your critique**.

Be solution-oriented.

Focus on actionable solutions instead of what you disagree with.

The reason for this tenet is the realization that you simply cannot change many people's minds. Diplomatically, this puts matters at a **standstill**, and many people often cannot move past it.

But what if you were to just 'agree to disagree,' and focus on treating the symptoms that make people feel badly? Maybe the internal intent can't or won't change, but at least the parties involved can find more peace and resolution if there is a compromise.

The clear answer is to focus on actionable solutions that will alleviate the problem.

Start with what resolution each party wants from the confrontation or criticism. Figure out primary and secondary motivations behind their actions and wants – this way you can understand which solutions will actually make them feel better.

From there, it is possible to create a list of possible solutions and resolutions, until one resonates with both parties as acceptable. This is not a process that would be possible if you had focused on an impasse between you two.

Indeed, sometimes it is far more productive to not even address the underlying issues if you do not think either party will actually change, and just seek to make them happier through solutions.

Countless friendships have been destroyed by unhealthy and misguided confrontation.

Part of social success is dealing with uncomfortable situations in smooth and graceful ways. Indeed it can mean a difference between preserving a friendship and destroying one. Much of this book has focused on positive conversations, but equally present are negative situations we cannot turn away from.

16. Listen to open them up.

Just because you are able to **hear** what somebody else is saying doesn't necessarily mean you are **listening** to them.

Listening involves more than just processing the sound waves that enter your ear canal.

Effective listening should enable you to clearly understand the motivations behind what a person is saying, and contribute in ways that will solve their problems or make them feel better about themselves. At least, this is the ideal goal.

Here are a few ways that you can improve your listening skills to not only increase your conversation skills, but to get people to open up to you like they would a close friend.

Compliment.

Make sure you communicate your appreciation for the fact that this person took the time, effort, and bother to share what he or she would like to share. This is very important because it sets the listening process and interpersonal communication process off on the right foot. When you fail to compliment the speaker, you're basically sending out a signal that this might be a confrontational or tense situation. That's hardly an ingredient for effective listening.

Create a safe space.

One of the biggest reasons that people are not as forthcoming as they would be otherwise is because they don't feel safe.

It's not a feeling of danger like swimming with sharks, but rather they don't feel **safe from judgment**. They imagine that people might think they are a bad person just for speaking their mind, or for personal opinions they hold.

And that's valid, because most of us do judge people fully and completely before we ever should.

So part of effective listening will hinge on your ability to create a safe and judgment-free space for people to really spill their guts and tell you what's on their mind.

This is a process that most of us are not used to, so here are a few guidelines to creating a space that will make people feel comfortable in opening up.

1. Don't show negative emotions when people express their personal opinions or thoughts. At worst, keep a

poker face. This shows that you don't disapprove of them or their choices.
2. Reveal aspects about yourself that might be judged by other people. If you do this and make yourself equally vulnerable, it will inspire others to share with you, assuming that you do not judge about such things.
3. Tell them explicitly that you do not judge, and realize that people's choices are their own and don't make them any better or worse of people.

Determine the main message.

This is a crucial part of effective listening.

When people talk, they aren't always very organized or articulate in their thoughts. Add that to emotional distress, and people are typically all over the place.

However, people are talking to you because something matters to them. There's a reason that they are sharing that particular piece of information – determine what that reason and underlying motivation is. Determine the main message and you can dig deeper into something that matters more deeply to them.

Don't interrupt.

Another thing to keep in mind when you're dealing with somebody who expresses a body language that communicates high level of engagement is to avoid talking over them. They're running downhill, and that's a **train** that is difficult to stop – and when you do stop it, it's both annoying and leaves a sour feeling.

When you're talking over somebody, it can be interpreted as a threatening gesture.

So make sure that they enough time to fully explain what they're saying and to fully communicate what they have to say, and then you ask follow-up questions or you share your own story. Avoid talking over them because you're not in a debate. You're not there to dominate. You're not there to intimidate people. **You're there to get people's trust and confidence**.

By following the steps here, you can go a long way in being perceived as a conscientious sincere listener.

Listening at its root is an exercise where you become closer to someone by hearing their narrative and relating to it yourself. However, most people have roadblocks in actually sharing their narrative that you must first overcome, and that's what I hope you have learned to overcome in this chapter.

Listening by itself is an easy act, but the path to effectiveness is more difficult than one would expect.

17. Digitally speaking.

If we have enough trouble communicating our intents face to face when we can see someone, just how much of that overall message do you think is lost when we communicate by digital means?

Okay, we're in an age now where most of our daily communication with friends is not by actually seeing them.

It's e-mail, texting, instant messaging, and any number of social media avenues.

While we can debate back and forth the value of relying on these kinds of communication, and whether or not it erodes our overall ability to communicate effectively... the fact of the matter remains that it is here to stay, and will only grow more prevalent.

Which means that we should think about our conversation skills and how to maximize them within digital means – which for my definition and the purposes of this chapter, includes phone, e-mails, chatting, and texting. The dynamics are simply different, and you cannot confuse what works on one medium with what works in another.

Remember that most of the message that we communicate isn't through the words that we say or speak, so you need to make your message **extra clear** over digital means. In fact, that leads me to my first point.

<u>If in doubt, make it 100% crystal clear.</u>

Without the benefit of all the signals that we usually utilize with in-person communication, part of our message is bound to get lost in the shuffle. Worse yet is when your message is completely misunderstood, and gets twisted into something that you have said nothing near.

Think about it – we've all done the same to others. "What did he mean 'I'll see you later?'" Are they being passive-aggressive, trying to be funny, sarcastic, or just oblivious?

What a simple smile or gesture might convey is completely lost over chat or e-mail. Therefore, if you are ever in doubt of the message you are sending, make 100% crystal clear of the intent to the other person.

You shouldn't feel awkward about this at all, because here's the alternative: your best friend assuming that you don't want to help them move, when in fact you were making a light-hearted joke about getting paid in pizza. Sound familiar or relatable?

Taking a quick aside and clarifying your message and intent to others will always be less painful and easier than you think – and of course, the upside as avoiding huge misunderstandings is priceless.

Key phrases:

1. Wait, you know I was just kidding, right?
2. Okay, that was a weird joke, but I actually meant [_____]...
3. By the way, I was kidding about that.
4. Boy, I need to be more clear about what I mean...

Smile when you're on the phone.

There's a reason that big business meetings are always insisted to be face-to-face.

When you meet someone in person, you get the words out of their mouths, their facial expressions, tone of voice, and body language. Obviously, three of those are lost with digital communication.

So while things might look good in writing through digital means, they might be saying something completely different unknowingly. Lacking a three dimensional view of a simple statement is dangerously incomplete, especially when important issues are at play.

A conversation by phone is universally recognized as the next best alternative to being able to see someone to communicate. The best way to avoid any kind of miscommunication, especially if it is a difficult subject matter or your humor skews mean, is to speak with a smile in your voice.

This means that when you're on the phone with someone, to imagine that they are right there in front of you and actually smile and emote. This is going to do two things.

First, when most of us talk on the phone, we emote less because we don't have anything visual to **react** to. This means that our voices also emote less, and less of the message we want to convey shines through. Smiling while you speak on the phone fixes this problem to a degree.

For practice, start taking your phone calls while you watch yourself in the mirror. Notice the difference.

Second, studies have shown time and time again that our minds can literally follow what our bodies do. This means that if you smile, you can **literally improve your overall mood**. This is beneficial for your conversation and your day in general.

Exaggerate your emotions.

In the absence of communication signals other than our words at face value, we latch onto other things that might indicate emotion and tone of voice – what people are thinking.

We can use this knowledge wisely, and exaggerate the emotions we want to convey to make sure that they are known. This is the difference between a wry smile and a chuckle, and an audible laugh punctuated by a "That's hilarious!"

If this feels fake to you, it shouldn't. In fact, it's the opposite – it's incredibly **honest**. All you're doing is making sure that people know how you honestly feel!

How else can you exaggerate your emotions? Aside from more loudly and directly reacting to what people say, you can outright say how you are feeling about something – that takes all the guesswork out of it.

For example, someone makes you mad. In person, you might frown, roll your eyes, and sigh loudly. How might you express the same over text or e-mail? There are a few ways, but each can be misinterpreted in a number of ways – the best way might simply be to directly express your emotion by saying "That was a little offputting the way you said that..."

Using emoticons 10% more than you currently do can also help with direct expression and making sure that no messages are mixed or missed.

The main theme of digitally speaking is to make sure that you are **conveying what you think you are**. We have enough trouble when we are staring someone right in the eye, so we must take extra care and caution when communicating over any other medium. It's worth noting that nothing in this chapter is a departure from other conversation skills that I have imparted to you – you should still integrate those, but simply ensure that you are being crystal clear about them.

18. A 21-day conversation bootcamp plan.

Just in case you were wondering... internalizing these conversation and social skills is a lifelong process.

Having the tools and knowledge is undoubtedly the first part of the required work, but it's less than half the battle as opposed to actually **applying and practicing** them. The mere preamble, so to speak.

Unfortunate yet is the fact that if you were to compare your social and conversation skills with other people's, they will inevitably develop at different rates as a result of our life experiences and innate abilities.

Yet the point is that they will improve given time and practice. For some more than others, it just might require a more regimented and structured plan – how about a 21 day conversation bootcamp plan?

<u>Day 1: Identify and understand your most common conversation problems.</u>

I don't care like how social you are. Everybody has a conversation **problem or sticking point**.

Maybe you end conversations too abruptly. Maybe you have a tough time starting conversations in the first place, or you just have a tough time maintaining conversations.

Regardless of the problem, there's always a solution to it. However, you're not going to arrive at a solution if you first don't identify the problem that you're grappling with. There's a reason why you keep running into the same road blocks again and again.

It's a good idea for Day 1 of this 21-day plan to sit down, and honestly figure out what your most common conversation problems are. This will also be useful in terms of **measuring your improvement**. Take note of the problems you have, and see how you feel about them on day 21.

Days 2 to 3: Note where conversations can be saved or extended.

There are common reasons that conversations end quickly or prematurely. When you spend days 2 to 3 observing and taking note of your interactions with other people, you will begin to see very distinct **patterns**.

Nobody is expecting you to be perfect. However, you just need to work on clearly identifying the good and bad things that happen in your conversations, otherwise what is the purpose and how can you learn?

Attempt to focus on what happens **right before** you say goodbye to someone and part ways, what happens **right before** an awkward silence, and what happens **right** *after* you greet someone.

Those are the three aspects of a conversation that can be worked on and improved, because they are the three spots where conversation can easily break down and wither away.

Spot any behavioral or conversational patterns you can, and start working on correcting them.

Days 4 to 7: Starting conversations smoothly.

Now that you have a clear idea as to why your conversation tends to end up working out or nor working out a certain way; the next step is to learn how to start conversation smoothly.

The good news is that people are looking to talk. They like talking about themselves, and they are more open to talking to people than you would expect.

We're in a constant search for an audience. You have to make this fact work to your advantage, and the good news is that starting conversations must focus on shared experiences.

What kind of common experiences can most people agree on? This will depend on what you do and who you see in your daily life.

For example, you're an engineer working in a big city.

You might expect the following types of topics for him: work, programming, commute, weather, lunch choices, weekend plans, projects, city events, upcoming vacation plans, siblings, family, pets... the list goes on.

These are all common experiences you have with the people around you. Starting a conversation is as easy as asking in an off-hand way about any of those topics.

"Did you hear that it was going to be super nice this weekend?"

"Didn't your brother just get married?"

"Can't believe we had to work 80 hours last week, right?"

"So I hear that the festival this weekend is going to have a lot of naked people..."

Days 8-9: Leaving smoothly.

Just as it takes skill to start a conversation smoothly, it also takes skill to end one on a good note. The worst thing you can do is to drop the ball and just have it cut off abruptly.

The whole point in engaging in conversations is really to know each other better and to feel better about each other. When you engage in conversations in such a way that you're cutting off people abruptly, this hardly leads to a positive place, especially if they haven't fulfilled one of the main purposes of a conversation: entertainment, information, or pleasure.

So learn the skills that you need to end conversations smoothly. Usually, this involves opening up the opportunity for future discussions. It can also involve setting up an appointment for a follow-up in the future.

Days 10 to 14: Going deeper.

As I've mentioned earlier, people don't really need much encouragement to talk about themselves.

But there are certain levels that people are accustomed to talking to, and most of these levels don't really build the relationships that you would want.

For what we want to accomplish with each conversation, we need to go deeper into topics and ultimately into people's lives and thoughts.

How do we do this? A few simple steps and mindsets to

embody.

Get personal. People are rarely as offended or violated as you think they might be, so the first lesson is to eradicate the mindset that you will offend people. Of course, this is something that should obviously be wielded with caution and common sense, but being 'safe' in a conversation will rarely lead anywhere revelatory.

Ask why. If you keep asking why, it forces people to explain their thoughts and intentions behind their actions. If you dig deep enough on the "whys" you will eventually begin to understand what drives a person and why they are who they are. It's a simple step, but powerful when used correctly and repeatedly.

Finally, **be bold**. This is the first point restated in somewhat of a different light. If you can't easily adopt the mindset of asking personal and more intimate questions of people, then you must start with attempting to be bold in your conversation topics.

Days 15 to 18: Non-verbal focus.

It's been said at least a few times in this book that most of the communication signals we end up actually sending aren't from the words we speak.

Therefore, it would make perfect sense to spend a few days focusing on how to read them, and subsequently how to display it.

Here's your task for days 15 to 18. Be a **master observer** – more than you were earlier in the 21 day period. This time, just grab a cup of coffee, and sit in a busy café.

You're going to choose a spot where you can easily see people go in and out and interact with each other. Hopefully, you can also spot a few awkward coffee dates along the way, which will be perfect for our purposes.

Then you're going to simply sip your coffee and watch people.

Start simple, and see if you can tell if an interaction or conversation is going well or poorly. What little facial expressions or gestures would make you feel this way? **Can you articulate why**?

From there, see if you can start to deduce the actual moods of the people involved. Are they happy, angry, sad, annoyed, joyous, nervous, or anxious? Can you articulate why?

Just make sure people don't catch you staring at them!

Days 19 to 20: Practice begins.

You've prepared for this for almost 3 weeks! This is when you can really begin internalizing the lessons learned, and put them into practice to solidify them.

The best people to practice with are the **service people** in your life – I mean the baristas, cashiers, and valets that we interact with on a daily basis.

These people are literally paid to be nice to you, and you have probably made their day far less boring just by engaging them.

Finally, it's a zero-risk move to practice on service people because there's a good chance that you won't see these people again in your life. If you crash and burn, which is unlikely given their jobs, then you have still lost nothing because they will not impact your life in any way.

Best to practice on people like that, that will have no impact on your life, than to dive in and practice with the CEO of your company at a big company networking event. It's **low-risk, high-reward**, and ultimately a satisfying thrill.

Day 21: Shoot for the moon.

Is there a challenging social situation that you have always been hesitant to face? Someone that you have always been hesitant to engage in conversation?

Now is the time to seize that fear and make an opportunity of it. You've honed your skills through smart study and practice for the past 3 weeks, so there is literally no point in your life that you have been more prepared for it.

The baristas may be too easy for you now, so it's time to put your skills to the challenge by tackling something big. The baristas also don't induce the anxiety or adrenaline that you'll feel on a daily basis in actual social situations that have some stakes, so it's time to start introducing those into your context and get used to besting them.

This challenge will be easier than you thought, and remember those problems you wrote at the beginning of the 21 days? Take a look at those and see how you feel about them now.

Make no mistake about it, great conversationalists are made. They are never born. You can be a social person, but you still need skills to build on your natural abilities to truly become a great conversationalist. Even if you're a true introvert and the thought of meeting and talking to strangers scares you, you can still develop the skill set you need to be an effective conversationalist.

19. Humor 101.

Whether or not you are a fan of standup comedy, you can't not acknowledge that there are comedians that are clearly superior to others. The difference between a Dane Cook (so-so in my opinion) and a Louis C.K. (crude and hilarious in my opinion) is as big as the Grand Canyon, and it's in no small part due to their delivery and timing.

Why am I telling you this?

It's simply to bring awareness to the fact that even people who tell jokes for a living sometimes aren't great at humor.

Now, combine that with the fact that humor is pretty much the best social lubricant there is, and that jokes are essentially short stories that are designed to produce specific responses. What do we get?

Humor, though supremely difficult, is damn important to daily conversation.

Luckily, scientists have actually studied humor and broken it down into small components that we can actually learn to use in daily conversation. More specifically, they have proposed that the vast majority of humor falls into a certain number of distinct patterns and structures, which I will introduce you to shortly.

Retitling.

This is when you reframe an action under a different name, usually in an exaggerated manner.

"Raj is walking in and out of traffic" becomes "Wow, Raj is embracing his inner Evil Kinevil."

"Did he just watch that terrible romantic comedy?" becomes "I guess he is trying to find his feminine side, huh?"

"He gets the same coffee every day" becomes "His blood is probably half latte these days."

Stating the opposite.

This is when you answer a question or statement with the opposite of the truth in a joking and often sarcastic manner.

"Who the hell was that?" "I'm guessing it wasn't Brad Pitt."

"Where does this road go to?" "Mordor, I think."

Underplaying impact.

This is similar to a euphemism – it is when you underplay the impact or damage made by something in a sarcastic manner. Some might recognize this as slightly passive-aggressive, but the key here is to not actually care about the impact and say it with a smile. This makes the other person know that the impact is not a big deal, and that you actually are joking.

"I'm sorry I didn't mean to hit you, are you okay?" "Totally ready to run a 5k, if you exclude my crushed foot and leg."

"I didn't mean for that e-mail to get sent out!" "Don't worry, it just upset the entire management team."

"Sorry I didn't wash the dishes." "No problem, I'm totally ready for invasion of the ants part two."

Emphasize the opposite of something shared.

This is where you take something that you share with the other person, and talk as if the opposite is true.

If it's a very cold day, "I'm going to go to the bathroom, let me know if I can get anyone some ice water or just ice cubes."

If it is a very sunny day, "Looks like we won't be getting tans today, guys."

If someone spills their drink, "And you can see why this place has won awards for cleanliness!"

<u>Literal observation.</u>

This is when you break something that you have observed down into very descriptive components.

On someone's butt: "It looks like two pringles hugging."

On a messy kitchen after cooking meat: "This looks like wolves have just fed."

On a bodybuilder's arms: "That bicep is literally the size of my head."

<u>An unexpected conclusion.</u>

This is when you are telling a story that seems to lead to a certain conclusion, but the conclusion you actually use is completely different from what they expect.

"I might not see my grandma again after this." "Is she okay?" "She's fine, I just don't like her very much."

"I really love walking to the beach." "You like the water a lot?" "No, I like watching surfers wipe out."

"I can't believe my dog is still alive." "Because he is so old?"

"More because he keeps stealing my chocolate."

So while some of these may be hit or miss for you, or may require some practice, these humor patterns and structures are literally scientifically proven to be funny.

Effective conversation is often bookended by humor, and if you can make someone simply laugh and enjoy themselves during a conversation, they will be that much more willing to stick around and continue it.

Not everyone has to be the life of the party, but laughter is incredibly disarming. It should be a formidable weapon in your arsenal, so embrace this and take some time to learn the structures and patterns I have presented.

Conclusion

Conversation – it's not always the stuff of Kissinger, but I hope it's been made clear exactly how much influence it can have on your daily life.

Without it, how are relationships built? More importantly, how are humans relatable to each other?

Conversation can easily be broken down into base elements and components, but it is not until you fit them all together that you will truly be able to master them.

This of course means that practice and application is integral to gaining the conversation skills that you desire. Some of you may need to stretch my 21 day plan in 42 or even 63 days, and that's okay.

Just make sure you are able to reflect on where you started, and it will be worth it already.

Sincerely,

Patrick King
Dating and Social Skills Coach
www.PatrickKingConsulting.com

P.S. If you enjoyed this book, please don't be shy and drop me a line, leave a review, or both! I love reading feedback, and reviews are the lifeblood of Kindle books, so they are always welcome and greatly appreciated.

Other books by Patrick King include:

CHATTER: Small Talk, Charisma, and How to Talk to Anyone http://www.amazon.com/dp/B00J5HH2Y6

Magnetic: How to Impress, Connect, and Influence http://www.amazon.com/dp/B00ON8WJKY

Social Fluency: Genuine Social Habits to Work a Room, Own a Conversation, and be Instantly Likeable... Even Introverts! http://www.amazon.com/dp/B00PJBF6JK

Cheat Sheet

1. MASTER CONVERSATION; RELATIONSHIPS. Becoming great at conversation will make people trust you, open up to you, and ultimately feel safe to you – three integral elements of strong friendships and relationships.

2. EVERYONE LIKES A VERBAL MIRROR. Reflect statements back towards people and make them the focus of the conversation to open them up and reach conversation depth.

3. ICEBREAKING, MELTING GLACIERS, AND STARTING A CONVERSATION. To effectively break the ice with anyone, use icebreakers that are related to something you share at the moment, and then lead the conversation back to them and focus on them.

4. COMMON QUESTIONS AND UNCOMMON, BETTER ANSWERS. Predict the common questions you will be asked on a day to day basis and prepare beforehand for interesting answers and mini-stories to jumpstart

interactions.

5. EFFECTIVE LISTENING IN THREE STEPS. Truly focus on the speaker, follow up with specific and pointed questions, and resist the urge to steal their thunder.

6. BUILDING A BULLETPROOF FIRST IMPRESSION. A truly effective first impression is holistic and includes your voice, body language, and how you carry the conversation's first sixty seconds.

7. TELL STORIES LIKE HOMER AND AESOP COMBINED. A story is ultimately an emotional experience, so beyond fulfilling the mechanical storytelling components, make sure that the listener is invested and that the emotional payload delivers.

8. MAKING SAFE TOPICS INTO FAILSAFE CONVERSATIONS. Most of the time it doesn't matter where you start a conversation from, as long as you can guide it into a personal and more intimate space.

9. AVOID AWKWARD AND UNCOMFORTABLE SILENCES. Conversation silences are typically caused by the lack of a leader in the conversation, so take that role and take responsibility to pre-empt each silence with deep or callback questions.

10. BODILY SPEAKING. Human comunication has very little to do with what we actually say, and far more to do with

how we deliver that message through our body and other non-verbal signals.

11. SOCIAL CUES SAY MORE THAN YOUR WORDS. Social cues are how people say what they really want to say, without having to say it. Often, the difference between recognizing certain cues is the difference between being extremely likeable and that person that everyone wants to avoid.

12. EXITING CONVERSATIONS WITH GRACE. Conversations typically serve three purposes to people, and as long as you give people the chance to feel somewhat fulfilled in one of the purposes, you should feel free to walk away.

13. CONVERSATION KILLERS. Conversations are typically cut short when they aren't given the chance to develop, or you don't let them.

14. IT'S AN INTROVERT'S PARTY TOO. Introverts are all about conserving and using their social batteries wisely, so passive participation and specific assumptions can help them rally for when they are spent.

15. CONFRONTING WITHOUT CONFRONTATION. Confrontation has torn many a relationship and friendship apart, so it is important to figure out ways to deliver negative messages without inflicting insult or injury.

16. LISTEN TO OPEN THEM UP. Listening effectively can

instantly transport you into close friend territory, and the main barrier to this is the fear of judgment and a lack of safe space to be vulnerable.

17. DIGITALLY SPEAKING. The main issue with most digital forms of communication is the lack of clarity, so exaggeration and explicit clarification will help you avoid misunderstandings.

19. HUMOR 101. Laughter is the best social lubricant that doesn't involve illicit substances, so focusing on a few patterns that humor typically follows will make you more likeable and engaging instantly.

63715070R00066

Made in the USA
Lexington, KY
15 May 2017